Do You KNOW?™

CHICAGO

A challenging little quiz about the amazing people, great places, and illustrious history of the Second City

Guy Robinson

SOURCEBOOKS, INC.®
NAPERVILLE, ILLINOIS

Copyright © 2008 by Carlinsky & Carlinsky, Inc.
Cover and internal design © 2008 by Sourcebooks, Inc.
Cover photo © iStockphoto.com/Steve Geer,
iStockphoto.com/Jim Jurica, and
iStockphoto.com/Joanna Pecha

All rights reserved. No part of this book may be reproduced in any
form or by any electronic or mechanical means including
information storage and retrieval systems—except in the case of
brief quotations embodied in critical articles or reviews—without
permission in writing from its publisher, Sourcebooks, Inc.

All brand names and product names used in this book are
trademarks, registered trademarks, or trade names of their
respective holders. Sourcebooks, Inc., is not associated with any
product or vendor in this book.

Published by Sourcebooks, Inc.
P.O. Box 4410, Naperville, Illinois 60567-4410
(630) 961-3900
Fax: (630) 961-2168
www.sourcebooks.com

Printed and bound in the United States of America
SP 10 9 8 7 6 5 4 3 2 1

If you live in a place for a while, or visit often, you might be surprised how much you pick up about its people, places, and things, about its local history and expressions, movies and songs, politicians and music makers, museums and comedy clubs, stadiums and suburbs, slogans and snacks—the many parts of the whole. Of course, you might also be surprised at what you *haven't* learned.

In this quiz on all things Chicago you'll find questions in both categories. Some are easy. Some will give even a native trouble. Of course, one person's "That's simple!" can be another's "Huh?" The questions are all over the lot, so it's fun to try them alone or with others.

One thing that's pretty certain: Everyone who submits to the test—home-grown, transplant, or frequent visitor—will meet some stumpers. Even if you breeze through the first few questions you look at, get ready for some head scratching. And maybe you'll learn a thing or two.

So here are 100 questions. Count ten points for each correct answer. Where a question has more than one part, you'll be told how to divide the credit. Here and there you'll find a chance to earn five or ten bonus points, so it's theoretically possible to score more than 1,000. (But you won't!)

Figure your performance this way:

Above 900:	**Spectacular!**
700–899:	A very solid showing
500–699:	Nothing to be ashamed of
Below 500:	Told you it was tough

R0414196786

CHICAGO PUBLIC LIBRARY
JEFFERY MANOR BRANCH
2401 E. 100th ST.
CHICAGO, IL 60617
312-747-6479

1. For almost any Chicagoan, what body parts does Magikist Carpet and Rug Cleaners bring to mind?

_____

2. Which did the city have as mayor first, an African American or a woman?

_____

3. Chicagoan Scott Turow, author of legal thrillers, is also a:

   a. Fireman
   b. Lawyer

   c. TV station owner
   d. Gun dealer

4. A crowd is filing into the building at 1058 West Washington Street (corner of Carpenter). Who's inside? (Hint: The name of one of the Marx Brothers is on the sign out front.)

_____

5. The Chicago tradition of meeting "under the clock" refers to what clock?

_____

6. For five points each, which of these roads is formally called a freeway, not an expressway or a tollway, and which has reversible express lanes?

a. Dan Ryan

b. Eisenhower

c. Bishop Ford

d. Kennedy

e. Stevenson

f. Elgin-O'Hare

g. Edens

h. Kingery

7. Where in Chicago did the Grateful Dead's final concert take place? (For five bonus points: The date was July 9. What year?)

_____

8. What kind of public art is seen often in Pilsen?

a. Fountains

b. Murals

c. Sculpture

d. Sidewalk chalk art

e. Decorative traffic lights

9. How does Chicago-style softball differ from softball everyplace else?

a. The ball is bigger and softer.

b. The ball is smaller and harder.

c. The batter uses two bats at once.

d. Base runners circle the infield clockwise.

10. Fill in the blanks in Carl Kassel's regular introduction to the one-hour news quiz radio program from NPR and Chicago Public Radio, *Wait Wait…Don't Tell Me!* "And here's your host at _____ _____ _____in downtown Chicago, Peter Sagal."

11. "Second City" and "The Windy City," sure. (And you know, of course, that the latter moniker has nothing to do with breezes from the Lake.) But here's a list of other nicknames for Chicago. Which of them is the official city motto, appearing (in Latin) on the corporate seal?

    a. "Gem of the Prairie"
    b. "The City That Works"
    c. "City of the Big Shoulders"
    d. "City in a Garden"
    e. "The 'I Will' City"

12. And who famously called Chicago "Hog butcher for the world"?

_____

13. Fill in the missing word in the *Tribune's* unfortunate headline of November 3, 1948: "DEWEY_____TRUMAN."

14. For five points each, pronounce:

    a. Mozart Street:_____

    b. Devon Avenue: _____

15. Once upon a time, a single area code covered the entire Chicago area. Those were the 312 days. Which was the first new code, added in 1989?

    a. 708
    b. 630
    c. 847
    d. 815

16. In 1987, A_____ L_____ moved from the *Sun-Times* to the *Tribune*.

17. The Chicago architect who said "Form ever follows function" designed the old Carson's building. The Chicago architect who said "Less is more" did the Chicago Federal Center. The Chicago architect who said "Nature is my manifestation of God" worked on the Rookery. Three points if you get one, six points for two, ten points for naming all three.

Carson's: _____

Federal Center: _____

The Rookery: _____

18. Which music group was *not* formed in Chicago?

    a. ABBA
    b. Styx
    c. Earth, Wind & Fire
    d. The Smashing Pumpkins

19. At what Chicago restaurant can you book a table in the kitchen?

    _____

20. The Aon Center is clad in white granite. When built, however, it was notably sheathed in slabs of_____.

21. Which business *didn't* get its start in Chicago?

    a. Wrigley   d. Crate & Barrel
    b. Sears, Roebuck   e. Tootsie Roll
    c. Dr. Scholl   f. International Harvester

22. For five points apiece, what two old Chicago public spaces were honored in 2001 with a U.S. postage stamp? (Hint: One is on the South Side, one on the North. The one on the South has been replaced.)

South: _____

North: _____

23. About how high above sea level is most of Chicago?

    a. 600 feet   c. 200 feet
    b. 400 feet   d. 100 feet

24. What are "the corncobs" and, for five extra points, what old TV series showed them in the backdrop of the opening scene each week?

_____

25. Which of these TV series *didn't* have a Chicagoland setting?

    a. *Webster*   e. *Joanie Loves Chachi*
    b. *Family Matters*   f. *Punky Brewster*
    c. *Good Times*   g. *ER*
    d. *Cosby*   h. *Married…With Children*

26. For five points each, what do Chicago people mean when they use these initials?

    a. LSD: _____

    b. The UC: _____

27. What Chicago periodical uses a backwards "R" as a logo?

_____

28. What's "The Hillside Strangler" to Chicagoans?

    a. A serial killer from the '70s who was never caught
    b. A super-hot stretch of highway in the western suburbs
    c. A Tex-Mex restaurant that serves killer chili
    d. A garage rock band made up of ex-wrestlers

29. Whose slogan is this? "Fresh to your family from _____."

30. What burger chain supposedly modeled its restaurant buildings after the Chicago Water Tower?

_____

31. If you're in a residential Chicago neighborhood on a winter day and see a couple of lawn chairs—or maybe a card table and a few milk crates—at the side of the street, what's going on?

_____

32. The Chicago Symphony Orchestra's founding conductor died a month after Orchestra Hall was opened. Who was he?

    a. Frederick Stock
    b. Fritz Reiner
    c. Theodore Thomas
    d. Karl Muck

33. If you see a sign reading:

> **WARNING**
> UNAUTHORIZED VEHICLES WILL BE
> RELOCATED AT OWNERS EXPENSE

who probably posted it?

_____

34. Who was Slats Grobnik?

_____

35. Five points for each phone number you can sing:

    a. Luna: _____

    b. Empire: _____

36. Which condiment is *never* applied to a Chicago-style hot dog?

    a. Mustard   e. Tomato

    b. Ketchup   f. Pickle

    c. Relish   g. Sport peppers

    d. Onion   h. Celery salt

37. For five points each:

    a. Where can you find hot-dog-shaped bubble gum? _____

    b. Where will you see two giant hot dog mascots named Maurie and
       Flaurie? _____

38. On December 2, 1942, as part of the Manhattan Project, scientists set off the first nuclear chain reaction under the stands of the University of Chicago's old Alonzo Stagg Field, which had been abandoned after the school dropped its football program a few years earlier. What's on the spot now?

_____

39. Five points for each onetime Chicago notable whose nickname you recognize.

    a. "Sweetness": _____

    b. "The Refrigerator": _____

40. Where do they do things they don't do on Broadway? The complete answer is six words: "_____ _____ _____

    _____ _____ _____ ."

41. According to a 1960s novelty number by Dr. West's Medicine Show and Junk Band, what alien vegetable visited Chicago, and what did it do to the city? (The song's title tells all.)

_____

42. One of these statements about Arnie Morton, founder of the restaurant chain, is *not* true. Pick it out.

    a. He got his first work experience in his father's South Side restaurant.
    b. He played football at University of Alabama.
    c. He was a key player in establishing Hugh Hefner's Playboy Club.
    d. He was instrumental in launching the yearly "Taste of Chicago" festival.
    e. He insisted on sweet relish and mustard with his steak.

43. What's the name of the Tyrannosaurus rex fossil skeleton at the Field Museum? (Ten point bonus: Where did the skeleton come from?) _____

44. Five points for each of these:

   a. Who was shot by the FBI at the Biograph Theater?

   _____

   b. The Saint Valentine's Day Massacre involved Al Capone's South Side gang and the North Side band led by:

   _____

45. The call letters WGN are widely known to stand for the immodest "World's Greatest Newspaper" label the *Trib* awarded itself. Five points each if you know the meaning of these:

   a. WLS: _____

   b. WVON: _____

46. How about these public television stations' call letters? Again, five points apiece.

   a. WTTW: _____ _____ _____ _____

   b. WYIN: _____ _____ _____ _____

47. Just one of these Chicago-area zoos charges admission. Which?

   a. Brookfield   c. Lincoln Park
   b. Cosley   d. Phillips Park

48. Bushman was a celebrated resident of Lincoln Park Zoo. What kind of animal was Bushman?

    a. Boa constrictor
    b. Chimpanzee
    c. Gorilla
    d. Macaw

49. What did John D. Rockefeller describe as "the best investment I ever made"?

_____

_____

50. Before the original Billy Goat Tavern became known for the *Saturday Night Live* "Cheezborger, cheezborger, cheezborger ... No Coke—Pepsi!" skit, the place was already famous for its role in the Cubs Curse and as a hangout for:

    a. Blues musicians
    b. Newspaper reporters
    c. Medical researchers
    d. Philosophy professors and students

51. What's the address reference in the Rolling Stones song title, "2120 South Michigan Avenue"?

    a. A record shop
    b. A record label
    c. A barber shop
    d. A head shop

52. Finish the Chicago Wolves' attack line: "We Play Hockey the Old-Fashioned Way:

    a. ...We Try Harder"
    b. ...We Actually Win"
    c. ...Without Any Padding"
    d. ...With a Steel Puck"

53. It's a window arrangement consisting of a large, fixed central pane with smaller double-hung windows on either side. What's it called?

_____

54. What do followers of Ike and followers of Rudy still argue about, decades later? (Hint: It may seem cheesy, but the dispute goes deep.)

_____

55. What happened to the Chicago Eight? (Twenty bonus points if you can name all eight.)

_____

_____

56. In what Chicago neighborhood can you see a tall statue of a man carrying a suitcase held together with string?

_____

57. And where can you find a statue of a guy wearing huge eyeglasses and holding a microphone?

_____

58. What's the title of the Picasso sculpture at Daley Plaza?

_____

59. What high-stakes thoroughbred horse race began in a Chicago
    suburb in 1981 with a win by Willie Shoemaker riding John Henry?

_____

60. What Chicago personality was noted for his regular use of
    expressions like "Oh, boy!" and "Hey, hey!"

_____

61. What cultural icon with a creamy filling was concocted by a
    Chicago bakery man in 1930?

_____

62. On which floor is the observation deck of the John Hancock Center?
    a. 94th   c. 96th
    b. 95th   d. 100th

63. What Oak Park native son described his home village as "a place
    of wide lawns and narrow minds"?

_____

64. For two points each, match the name to the type of institution it graces:

a. Adler
b. Shedd
c. Notebaert
d. Newberry
e. Guy

f. nature museum
g. research library
h. planetarium
i. blues club
j. aquarium

65. Where in Chicago can you see a famous painting of the artist's sister, his dentist, and a pitchfork?

_____

66. Where did Jane Byrne and her husband move for a few weeks in 1981 to highlight security troubles in public housing developments?

_____

67. How did Mayor Anton J. Cermak die?

_____

68. Arrange these Lake Michigan beaches from north to south:

- a. 12th Street
- b. Humboldt Park
- c. Rainbow
- d. Montrose Avenue
- e. North Avenue
- f. Oak Street
- g. Kathy Osterman
- h. South Shore

69. Could you be a Chicago postal carrier? Two points for each proper match:

- a. Wrigley Building
- b. Union Station
- c. Leo Burnett Building
- d. Drake Hotel
- e. The Pump Room

- f. 35 West Wacker Drive
- g. 210 South Canal Street
- h. 1301 North State Parkway
- i. 410 North Michigan Avenue
- j. 140 East Walton Place

70. Two mayors named Richard Daley, two middle names. Five points for each:

Son: Richard _____ Daley

Father: Richard _____ Daley

71. Which movie is *not* set in Chicago?

- a. *The Front Page*
- b. *The Sting*
- c. *Ferris Bueller's Day Off*
- d. *The Blues Brothers*

- e. *Mystic Pizza*
- f. *Little Caesar*
- g. *A Raisin in the Sun*
- h. *My Big Fat Greek Wedding*

72. Not one of these "Chicago writers" was born anywhere near Chicago. For two points each, match them with their birthplaces.

a. Studs Terkel
b. Nelson Algren
c. Saul Bellow
d. Bob Greene
e. Dave Eggers

f. Bexley, Ohio
g. Boston
h. Detroit
i. New York City
j. Lachine, Québec

73. What's on the site of the former O'Leary property, where the Great Fire of 1871 is said to have begun?

_____

74. Where in Chicago is the song "Na Na Hey Hey Kiss Him Goodbye" most often played regularly?

_____

75. What did University of Chicago senior Jay Berwanger do first? (Hint: He probably kept it on a shelf.)

_____

76. Who's noted for saying *"I've* got something for *you*!"

_____

77. Which terminal number is missing at O'Hare International Airport?

a. 1
b. 2
c. 3

d. 4
e. 5

78. The airport code for O'Hare is ORD. Why? (Five-point bonus: The man who gave his name to the airport, Butch O'Hare, was a decorated Navy flyer. In what war?)

79. How about Chicago Midway? What's the code for that one?

_____

_____

80. What local brewery makes, among others, Honkers Ale, India Pale Ale, and Oatmeal Stout?

_____

81. Who *isn't* counted among the alumni of The Second City?

    a. Joan Rivers
    b. John Belushi
    c. Jim Belushi
    d. Bill Murray
    e. Mike Myers

    f. Jon Stewart
    g. Chris Farley
    h. Steve Carell
    i. Stephen Colbert
    j. Tina Fey

82. Going eastbound on the Ike, where does the expressway end?

_____

83. At which local university was the rock band Chicago formed?

    a. Northwestern
    b. CSU
    c. IIT
    d. UIC

    e. Wheaton
    f. DePaul
    g. Loyola

84. What landmark structure, built in art deco style, looks like—and is said to have been inspired by—a champagne bottle?

_____

85. The old Playboy Mansion, at 1340 North State Parkway, is now:

   a. An office building
   b. A Crate & Barrel store
   c. Condos
   d. Playboy offices
   e. A parking lot

86. Who *wasn't* born in Chicago?

   a. Benny Goodman
   b. Michael Jordan
   c. Michael Crichton
   d. Pat Sajak

   e. Harrison Ford
   f. George Wendt
   g. Robin Williams
   h. Mr. T

87. What's the only building from the 1893 World's Columbian Exposition that has survived in place, and is today a National Historic Landmark?

_____

88. What Christmas story starring a beloved character known worldwide was created by a staff copywriter for a Chicago company as a promotional giveaway?

_____

89. What's a Chicago bankroll?

_____

90. And a Chicago piano?

91. Who was "The Father of
Chicago Blues"?

_____

_____

92. An Italian beef "combo" sandwich pairs
which of these ingredients with the beef?

    a. Raw beef
    b. Italian sausage
    c. Hot peppers
    d. Lasagna noodles

93. After being a Chicago fixture for decades, he died in 2003. His
tombstone calls him "Mr. Chicago," but everyone in town knew him
by a one-syllable nickname. Who was he?

_____

94. Why do many people say "Hi, Bob!" when they visit Navy Pier?

_____

95. Which statement about Lake Michigan *isn't* true?

    a. It's the largest fresh water lake in the country.
    b. Unlike the other four Great Lakes, it has no Canadian shore.
    c. Its name was chosen in an open contest in 1839; 8,000 entries were received.
    d. Its maximum depth is more than 900 feet.

96. The Chicago Harbor Lighthouse stands between two low buildings. What color are those buildings' roofs?

97. On what day of the year does the Chicago River change appearance?

98. Buckingham Fountain was modeled after a fountain in:

    a. Washington DC
    b. Versailles, France
    c. Bath, England
    d. Petra, Jordan

99. What Chicago business used the slogan "As Chicago as it gets"? (A hint you probably don't need: dark green awnings.)

_____

100. Name the former U.S. vice president who once greeted a Windy City audience with: "It's wonderful to be in the great state of Chicago."

_____

1. Lips (remember the Magikist flashing lips signs, which once graced several city expressways?)

2. A woman: Jane Byrne took office in 1979, Harold Washington in 1983

3. b.

4. Oprah (the building houses her Harpo Studios)

5. The one at the flagship Marshall Field's (now Macy's)

6. c. and d.

7. Soldier Field (bonus: 1995, shortly before Jerry Garcia died)

8. b.

9. a. (the ball is 16 inches around instead of 12 and soft enough that the game is often called "mushball"; fielders use their bare hands)

10. The Chase Auditorium

11. d. *(Urbs in Horto)*

12. Carl Sandburg (in the poem "Chicago")

13. DEFEATS

14. a. MO-zart (with a soft *z*), b. dih-VON

15. a.

16. Ann Landers

17. Carson's, Louis Sullivan; Federal Center, Mies van der Rohe; the Rookery, Frank Lloyd Wright

18. a.

19. Charlie Trotter's

20. Carrara marble

21. e. (the chewy candy was developed in New York City, but the company is now headquartered in Chicago)

22. South, Comiskey Park; North, Wrigley Field

23. a.

24. The twin towers of Marina City (extra: *The Bob Newhart Show*)

25. d.

26. LSD = Lake Shore Drive, the UC = United Center

27. *Chicago Reader*

28. b. (an interchange on the Eisenhower Expressway in the village of Hillside)

29. Jewel

30. White Castle

31. Someone's reserving a parking space

32. c.

33. Lincoln Towing Service (not the kind of towing service you can call if your car's water pump breaks; they're enforcers)

34. The fictional Chicago everyman created by columnist and author Mike Royko

35. "7-7-3, 2-0-2 (beep beep beep beep), LuNAAAA! (Ding!)"; "8-hundred, 5-8-8, 2-3-hundred, EmPIIIRE!"

36. b.

37. a. Fluky's, b. Superdawg

38. The university's main library, the Joseph M. Regenstein Library, known as "The Reg"

39. a. Chicago Bears running back Walter Payton, b. Bears defensive lineman William Perry

40. "On State Street, that great street" (from "Chicago," the song sung most famously by Frank Sinatra)

41. "The Eggplant That Ate Chicago" (and the lyric warned: "If he's still hungry, the whole country's doomed")

42. e.

43. Sue—named for Sue Hendrickson, the fossil hunter who made the find (bonus: South Dakota)

44. a. John Dillinger, b. Bugs Moran

45. a. "World's Largest Store" (after its original owner, Sears, Roebuck), b. at first "Voice of the Negro" but changed to "Voice of the Nation"

46. a. "Windows to the World", b. "We're Your Indiana Neighbor"

47. a.

48. c.

49. The University of Chicago, which he largely funded in 1890

50. b.

51. b. (it was the address of Chess Records, a key label in the blues and rock 'n' roll worlds)

52. b.

53. A Chicago window

54. It's a question of great historical importance: Who should get the credit for inventing deep-dish pizza, Ike Sewell of Pizzeria Uno or Rudy Malnati, who worked for Ike?

55. They were the group tried for conspiracy and inciting to riot at the 1968 Democratic National Convention—Bobby Seale was separated from the case for his own trial, leaving the better remembered Chicago Seven; after appeal of convictions handed down to some of the defendants, all eight were ultimately acquitted (bonus: Abbie Hoffman, Jerry Rubin, Tom Hayden, David Dellinger, Rennie Davis, John Froines, Lee Weiner, and Seale)

56. In Bronzeville, at 26th Place and Martin Luther King Drive (the sculpture portrays a newly arrived immigrant from the South during the "Great Migration" of the early 20th century)

57. At Wrigley Field (it's Harry Caray, of course)

58. It has none (which is why everybody calls it "The Picasso")

59. The Arlington Million, the horse racing world's first million-dollar event, now a yearly contest at Arlington Park Race Track

60. Sports broadcaster Jack Brickhouse

61. The Twinkie

62. a.

63. Ernest Hemingway

64. a.-h. (Adler Planetarium and Astronomy Museum), b.-j. (John G. Shedd Aquarium), c.-f. (Peggy Notebaert Nature Museum), d.-g. (Newberry Library), e.-i. (Buddy Guy's Legends)

65. You'll find Grant Wood's *American Gothic* at the Art Institute of Chicago

66. An apartment in the Cabrini-Green public housing project

67. In Miami, Florida, in 1933, he was mortally wounded by a gunman who had allegedly been aiming at president-elect Franklin D. Roosevelt

68. g., d., e., b., f., a., h., c.

69. a.-i., b.-g., c.-f., d.-j., e.-h.

70. Son Michael, father Joseph

71. e.

72. a.-i., b.-h., c.-j., d.-f., e.-g.

73. Chicago Fire Academy

74. At "The Cell," U.S. Cellular Field, during White Sox games

75. He won the first-ever Heisman Trophy as the nation's top college football player (although the award wasn't named the Heisman until the following year, after Heisman had died)

76. The guy in the bald eagle costume in commercials for Eagle Insurance

77. d. (terminal 4 closed in 1993)

78. In an earlier day, it was called Orchard Place Airport and Douglas Field (bonus: World War II)

79. MDW

80. Goose Island Brewery

81. f.

82. The old main Post Office building

83. f.

84. The Hard Rock Hotel Chicago (originally the Carbide & Carbon Building)

85. c.

86. b.

87. The Museum of Science and Industry

88. "Rudolph the Red-Nosed Reindeer" (the company was Montgomery Ward, the year 1939)

89. A wad of paper money made up of mostly singles with a $50 or $100 bill on top for show

90. A favorite Prohibition-era weapon, the Thompson submachine gun, or "Tommy gun"

91. The Mississippi-born Muddy Waters

92. b.

93. "Kup"—longtime daily newspaper columnist and TV talk show host Irv Kupcinet

94. Because they see the bronze sculpture depicting Bob Newhart as psychologist Robert Hartley, seated in a chair opposite his office couch

95. c.

96. Red

97. The day of the St. Patrick's Day Parade (March 17 or the Saturday before), when it's dyed fluorescent green

98. b.

99. Marshall Field's

100. Dan Quayle of Indiana